# SMILEYS

*Compiled by David W. Sanderson*

*Text by Dale Dougherty*

*O'Reilly & Associates, Inc.*

**Smileys**
Compiled by David W. Sanderson (dws@ssec.wisc.edu)
Text by Dale Dougherty and David W. Sanderson

Designed and Produced by
Jennifer Niederst and Edie Freedman

Interior illustrations by Jennifer Niederst
Cover design and illustration by Edie Freedman

ISBN: 1-56592-041-4                                    [3/00]
[C]

# What is a smiley?

A smiley is a sequence of ordinary characters you can find on your computer keyboard. Smileys are used in e-mail and other forms of communication using computers. The most popular smiley is a smiling face that people use to say "don't take what I just wrote too seriously."

```
Smileys are a very serious
subject! :-)
```

If you don't see that it represents a smiling face, tip your head to the left and look at it again. The colon represents the eyes, the dash represents the nose, and the right parenthesis represents the (smiling) mouth. There are smileys for sadness as well as delight.

Another term for smileys is "emoticons," which presumably means icons representing emotions.

# Why are smileys sideways?

Not all smileys are turned counterclockwise, but most of them are. A smiley is made up of characters on a computer keyboard, typed to fit on a single line. The smiley usually follows after the punctuation mark at the end of a sentence.

But there's another slant. Most people notice something sideways about the emotions expressed by smileys.

```
I meant to send flowers. ;-)
```

I can say something, and then wink at you. A smiley is a gesture that everything is cool, no matter what I say, because I know you'll understand.

```
I'm slowing down.
I don't look for
adventure anymore. :-)
```

I'm talking out of the side of my mouth. I can say something perhaps a bit cynical and then use a smiley to have a laugh and disavow it all at once.

Well, having no vacation simplifies my life quite a bit. :-(

A smiley tells someone what you really mean when you make an offhand remark.

# Style & Usage

*Smileys convey a broad range of emotions expressed sideways.*

## The Standard Smiley

You are joking.

You are satisfied.

This is the only smiley you know.

```
Why not make the same
mistakes everyone
else makes? :-)
```

```
How should I know? I
got it for free.   :-)
```

## The Sad Smiley

You aren't joking, sadly.

You are not satisfied.

This is the only other smiley you know.

```
I must have been typing
faster than I think. :-(
```

```
It has to be a bug in the
install program. :-(
```

```
Some fun.   :-(
```

## The Winking Smiley

You don't mean it, even
if you are joking.

"Surely you know what I mean."

You are being sardonic even if you don't
know what that means.

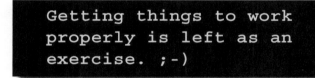

```
Getting things to work
properly is left as an
exercise. ;-)
```

## The Crying Smileys

You want to cry.

You could cry if you had to.

You are actually shedding tears.

You are bawling.

## The Confused Smileys

You don't know how you
feel but you'll let me know
in the morning.

You hope you don't feel as I do.

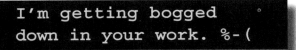

```
I'm getting bogged
down in your work. %-(
```

You don't know how you feel,
but then you don't feel bad.

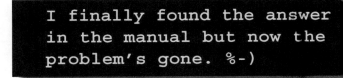

```
I finally found the answer
in the manual but now the
problem's gone. %-)
```

## The Shocked & Amazed Smileys

Uh-oh!

You don't believe you said that.

Ask me to tell you more.

```
He had the nerve to call
_me_ a nerd. :-o
```

O my god!

```
You can guess what I
said ( 8-o ) once I knew
I deleted your files.
```

## The Sarcastic Smileys

**: -]**

You are your own worst enemy.

```
I must have asked
people to flame me. :-]
```

```
If I had the time to
RTFM*, I wouldn't bother
you. :-]
```

**: - [**

You are your own best friend.

```
Sorry, nobody's home. :-[
```

*Read the F***ing Manual

## The Apathetic Smiley

You say so because you were told what to say.

You don't care what it means.

```
The opinions expressed
are not those of my
employer.  :-|
```

```
           Some joke.  :-|
```

## The Angry Smiley

You have reached your limit.

You are seething mad.

```
I'm new and I did not
deserve such heated respons-
es. :-||  It was just a sim-
ple
question, guys.
```

```
It's all a scam ( :-|| )
so I'll never believe what
they tell me anymore.
```

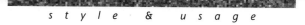

## The Invisible Smiley

"I don't know you well enough
to use smileys."

Have a nice day.

# Why use smileys?

Smileys allow you to express yourself. You can have fun with them.

Me, again. I know I'm pretty
hard to shut up :-()

The smileys in widest use are simple facial expressions, but their meaning is something personal, whatever you want them to mean. I can say something that I can't put into words, something that I can depend on you to understand. There are smileys that are simply clever caricatures.

Here's Uncle Sam:    =):-)

Here's a wizard:    -=#:-) \

Nobody uses caricatures as they do the basic smiley. But the endless variety of smileys is intriguing, and once you see so many of them, you can't resist the urge to create one of your own.

# Smiley Caricatures

5:-)   Elvis Presley

:-)B   Dolly Parton

:-O   Mick Jagger

:-.)   Madonna

:/7)   Cyrano de Bergerac

)   Cheshire Cat

O-)   Cyclops

```
=/:-)       Abe Lincoln

   :'}      Richard Nixon

 :(=)      Jimmy Carter

7:^]      Ronald Reagan

          George Bush

\|=//

      =:o]    Bill Clinton
```

```
 7:-)      Fred Flintstone

 8(:-)     Mouseketeer

   =^)      Dagwood Bumstead

->=:-)X    Zippy the Pinhead

 #:o+=     Betty Boop

 3  :-)    Bart Simpson

   >:*)     Bozo the Clown

   B-)      Batman

   =*0      Felix the Cat
```

# Where do people use smileys?

People use smileys primarily in electronic mail (e-mail) messages. They are also found in communication that takes place on electronic bulletin boards and forums such as Usenet, the informal news distribution system of computer networks. People use smileys in messages that they post to interest-specific newsgroups that are distributed around the world. Smileys are global travellers.

# Smiley Animals

| | |
|---|---|
| 8) | frog |
| 8:) | pig |
| 3:-o | cow |
| pp# | another cow |
| pq`#' | bull |
| .\/ | duck |
| 8^ | chicken |
| <:>== | turkey |

```
  := |     baboon

   :<=     walrus

   :V)     woodpecker

 >-^);>    fish

=====:}    snake

 ~~~~8}    another snake

    8:]    gorilla
```

3:]    basic pet smiley

>:]    another pet smiley

3:[    mean pet smiley

:3-<    dog

}:-<    cat

**People have communicated in writing for centuries without resorting to smileys. What makes writing e-mail messages different?**

Speed.

Writing a memo or letter on paper is very different from communicating by e-mail. In fact, using e-mail is closer to having a telephone conversation than writing a letter. It is almost immediate, decidedly informal, and potentially overwhelming.

E-mail writing is often written ``off the cuff,'' and each exchange is only one piece of an ongoing conversation. It holds great potential for miscommunication between both parties. The context of the conversation evolves rapidly, suddenly including new people and new perspectives, and can become quite complicated.

You often need to rely on personal expression to make up for any misunderstandings.

You might include a smiley as a reminder of the ongoing context of the conversation, to indicate that your words don't stand on their own. A smiley can point out to the other participants of the conversation that they need to understand you and your personality in order to understand what you've said.

```
I'm sure I've said enough.    :-)
```

# How frequently should I use smileys?

Like any punctuation mark, overuse marks you as a beginner. For instance, someone who uses five exclamation marks after a sentence, or who uses an exclamation mark after every sentence in the paragraph, runs the risk of having his readers ignore the exclamation marks entirely. It's a bit like Peter crying wolf too many times, or a piece of music consisting entirely of *fortissimo* without any *pianissimo* at all. If someone writes this way then I usually think he's either not too bright about punctuation marks, or writes advertising for a living. :-)

# Specialized Smileys

oCc:-)    Carmen Miranda

/:-)    with a beret

d:-)    with a baseball cap

=|:-)    Abe Lincoln

<:-)    dunce hat

*<8-)    party hat

=):-)    Uncle Sam

<<<<<(:-)    hat salesman

| | |
|---|---|
| `-:-)` | mohawk |
| `=:-)` | punk rocker |
| `#:-)` | with matted hair |
| `{:-)` | with hair parted down the middle |
| `,:-)` | with toupee |
| `y:-)` | with bad toupee |
| `}:-)` | with toupee in an updraft |
| `&:-)` | with curly hair |
| `?:)` | with single curl |
| `(-)` | needs hair cut |

```
:-(>~    with goatee

:-#|     bushy moustache

(:-{~    bald and bearded

|:-)     with bushy eyebrows

`:-)     with one eyebrow raised
```

```
d:-)    baseball player

q:-)    catcher

=:-H    football player
```

!-(   unhappy about black eye

   !-)   proud of black eye

%+{   lost a fight

   :+(   punched nose, hurt

@-)   seeing stars

## inebriated smileys

#-)      partied all night

%*}      very drunk

:*)      drinking every night

%-<I>    drunk with laughter

%-\      hungover

%*@:-(   so hungover my head
         hurts

| | |
|---|---|
| :-'\| | has a cold |
| :-~\| | also has a cold |
| %-6 | braindead |
| *-) | shot dead |
| X-( | just died |
| 8-# | death |

31

| | |
|---|---|
| :b | sticking tongue out |
| :d | same thing |
| :-q | trying to touch tongue to nose |
| :-w | speak with forked tongue |
| :>) | big nose |
| (:-D | blabber mouth |
| :-(O) | yelling |
| :-@ | cursing |

:-x     kiss, kiss

:-X     a big wet kiss!

:-<>    kissy faces

:*    kisses

(:-*    kissing

:-P    telling secrets

:X    lips are sealed

:-    male

>-    female

```
   3:*>      Rudolph the
             red-nosed reindeer

3:^> 3:^>   Donner, Blitzen

  *<|:-)     Santa Claus

    <:>      Elf

    <:^<     Grinch
```

## Department Store Santas

```
*<|:-)
*<|:-))
*<|:-{))
oO:-)***
o-<:-{{{
```

## Really Truly Santa

```
*<:-)
```

0:-)    angel

O 8-)    the angelic halo look

O :-)    an angel (at heart, at least)



>:)    a little devil

>:-)    devil

>:->    devilish

>;-)    devilish wink

>;->    winky and devil combined. A very lewd remark was just made.

C=>8*)    devilish chef with glasses and a moustache

```
  !.'v    flat top
*<.'v    wearing snow cap
+<.'v    knight
  ,.'v    has short hair
   .'!    grim
   .'"    pursing lips
   .'J    smiling
   .'P    sticking tongue out
   .'T    keeping a straight face
   .'U    yawning
   .'V    shouting
   .'Y    whistling
   .'\    frowning
   .'r    sticking tongue out
   .'v    talking
   .'w    speaking with
          forked tongue
   .^v    pointy nose
  =.'v    has mohawk
  @.'v    has curly hair
  d.'v    wearing hard hat
  ~'v     has long bangs
```

*Here are things you find in and around Smiley Town.*

| | |
|---|---|
| `oF-oo—-oo` | semi-truck |
| `==========` | railroad tracks |
| `^v^v^` | mountains |
| `/\___/\` | drawbridge |
| `[] [] [] [] []` | apartment complex |
| `\|$.$\|` | bank |
| `\|<S>\|` | comic bookstore |
| `<] [ [ [<` | fishmonger |
| `- - - -` | tailor |
| `[+/-]` | grade school |
| `` ` ~ ' ~ ' ~ ' ` `` | dance school |
| `_(—)_` | hamburger stand |
| `(_)]` | coffee shop |
| `[_W_]` | fortune teller |
| `(_<>_)` | jeweler |
| `}{}{}{` | hedges |
| `_i _i _i` | streetlamps |
| `&==& &==&` | park benches |
| `->-` | airport |

# Are smileys used outside of e-mail and bulletin boards?

I haven't mentioned a program called ``talk'' which allows you to communicate interactively with other people using the same computer. Depending on the system, you might even be able to use ``talk'' to communicate with people using other computers on a network. It works like this:

When a pair of people (call them Padruig and Ian) use a pair of ``talk'' programs to communicate, Padruig's ``talk'' program shows what Padruig types in the top half of Padruig's display, and it shows what Ian types in the bottom half of Padruig's display. Similarly, Ian's ``talk'' program shows what Ian types in the top half of Ian's display, and it shows what Padruig types in the bottom half of Ian's display. So, whenever either Padruig or Ian types anything, both of them see it.

This sort of communication can be very convenient. It can let you have a conversation when a data connection is

From: Barry
To: Larry

So, how's the weather in Wisconsin?

From: Larry
To: Barry

We've had the cloudiest November on record. I'm slowly going crazy since I haven't seen the sun in thirty days. %-{

From: Barry
To: Larry

Ah, then I expect I won't get too much sympathy for the miserably sunny weather here in Australia! :-)

readily available but a phone connection isn't. For instance, I recently used ``talk'' to have conversation with a friend of mine when he was at McMurdo base in Antarctica. A telephone connection was out of the question. But since the satellite data link was available, we could have a conversation using our computers.

In such interactive situations the same possibilities for misinterpretation in e-mail are even more apparent, since people tend to consider what they type at each other in a "talk" session even less carefully than they consider what they type at each other via e-mail. I use smileys more frequently when using "talk" than when I communicate via e-mail.

From: Jean
To: William

```
Whoops, I forgot
to buy light bulbs.
I'm really in the
dark today. %-)
```

From: William
To: Jean

```
That wasn't very
bright of you.:-)
```

## Smiley Comics

| :-) | 8-) | 8-{) |

A smiley to disguise himself gets glasses and a fake moustache.

| :-) | :-)~ | :-() | :-i(=) | :-9 |

A smiley begins drooling, opens wide to eat, chews it,
and then licks his lips.

| :-)— | :-)== | :-|== |

A 98 lb. weakling smiley gains a muscular build and loses his
good sense of humor.

| :-( | :-( ) | :-() |

A frowning smiley saw food and felt better.

| :-) | [:-) | <[:-) |

A smiley who has his head shaved wears a hat to avoid looking
like a blockhead.

| C:-) | >[] | c8-) |

A smart smiley left watching too much TV.

| <:-) | &:-) | 3:-) |

A smiley gets a perm that lasts only a few weeks.

| :-| | %-| | |-) |

A smiley worked all day and worked all night before finally getting some sleep.

| :-) | :-D | :-|) | :D | :-D D- |

A smiley starts laughing and can't stop himself.

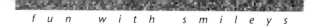

# Where's Smiley?

There are a lot of different smileys hidden in the lines of random characters below, but there's only one plain vanilla smiley. :-)

```
M20F/X$B27=_P5.@T$]RC`V`1W/3/&B?:-8
M)>BE#!%-\AS/M):HG%!JB8-LR_O&7@/[QI
M:WQLP\4_5$H;N9%Z-;-)O1:-3$%?+IV:F(
MX:P3AG":98)A@)9'-/Z!7HQ=4)Z%;XS3,&
M$O)=XHFRPI9NN>0JLN-7NL?S-G`Y<TM=5_
MH\)&M]13A"/+<YM3"$>$_O&WK:.L!+X`'\
MX"^[SK%$EB?5R"?H]O(:)-9>^C6K`*;NXI
M-,:SW=QK-C71I%[\*;.D/".D+*0;X'+?>I
MUBL)GTD-T\A#<]_:^')_R">R:_^:6WXM=Y
M_\A%EN$]L@5;(F+Y[!B.2^W]Z#JQ7YF>GR
MH9?.)2S&4*49RA=W:MYG>C!QEJW.),LOG)
M\K:\KR*Y[!Z#_76XO!=$X*>7&6GWO*5\\7
MM>F:7|7W9%#!YK[[>KEZV/8,JV-`XU<],4
MKH'V<`WF:,93SF5?WF6MM/6#@%V0S95(&=
M,LYH1='>2VC-/H2?74SA0C":"4H+\^3T\;
M&1<4;S%(:#5G%RA]!VR-H.QO-\$;]$BW;>
M8M;XR7?.#:OG"`^*&%HXM"*?0#?:-)F6#L
MGEQ3^@W1D4.R:)2I.XRZ/=36P/)0$F,0N_
MO$:NK^&KV:G&-H6=3:VF>SCIR(=S2NG-.-
M2-R`+:$S1H@Y3F()DQIG-',C?)RL[IZSN!
```

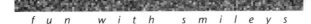

# Smiley Quiz

1. `*<:-)`              a. confused
2. `=^)`               b. frog
3. `[:-)`              c. wizard
4. `8=:-)`             d. Santa Claus
5. `8)`                e. Ronald Reagan
6. `%\v`               f. Mouseketeer
7. `-=#:-)`            g. Dagwood Bumstead
8. `8(:-)`             h. ha ha!
9. `%-(`               i. partied all night
10. `:-)`              j. chef
11. `#-)`              k. listening to walkman
12. `7:^]`             l. Picasso man

**Answers:**

1-d, 2-g, 3-k, 4-j, 5-b, 6-i, 7-c, 8-f, 9-a, 10-h, 11-i, 12-e

# Smiley Makeover

| BEFORE | AFTER |
|--------|-------|
| `:-|` | `&:-)` |
| `(-|` | `@:-)` |
| `|:o(` | `\:o)` |
| `7:-|` | `?:-)` |

# Faces in the Crowd

How many sad smileys do you see in the crowd?
How many winkey smileys do you see?
How many apathetic smileys do you see?

```
:-)   :-)   :-)   :-)   :-)   :-)   :-)
:-)   :-)   :-)   :-)   :-)   :-)   :-)
:-)   :-(   :-|   :-)   ;-)   :-)   :-)
:-)   :-)   :-)   :-)   :-)   :-)   :-)
:-)   :-)   :-)   :-)   :-)   :-)   :-)
:-)   :-)   :-)   :-)   :-)   :-)   :-)
:-)   :-)   :-)   :-)   ;-)   :-)   :-)
:-)   :-)   :-)   :-)   :-(   :-)   :-)
:-)   :-)   :-)   :-)   :-)   :-)   :-)
:-)   :-)   :-)   :-)   :-)   :-)   :-)
:-)   :-)   :-)   :-)   :-)   :-)   :-)
:-)   :-(   :-)   :-)   :-)   :-)   :-)
:-)   :-(   :-)   :-)   :-)   :-)   :-)
:-)   :-)   :-)   :-|   :-)   :-)   :-)
:-)   ;-)   :-)   :-)   :-)   :-)   :-)
:-)   :-)   :-)   :-)   :-)   :-)   :-)
:-)   :-)   :-)   :-)   :-)   :-)   :-)
:-)   :-)   :-)   :-)   :-)   :-)   :-)
;-)   :-)   :-)   :-)   :-)   :-(   :-)
```

# Since smileys contain punctuation marks, how do I mix them with the punctuation I use in my sentences?

In general, use them after the end of the regular sentence punctuation, instead of before it. This way, they act like pictographic sentences, and people won't confuse the regular punctuation with the characters in the smiley.

# What about parenthetical text?

If the smiley doesn't end with a ")", then just separate the smiley from the ")" with a space or two.

If the smiley *does* end with ")", then you can either use it to end the parenthetical text, or leave a couple of spaces after the smiley to separate it from the ")". I prefer the former, since I like balanced parentheses, but many people don't care one way or the other about it.

Both methods are in common use.

*The following list represents actual network usage. All kinds of people have created the smileys on this list. Not everyone shares the same sensibilities, so you may find some of the smileys dumb, tasteless, or even offensive. By their nature, smileys are stereotypes. This is a dictionary, not a recommendation for use.*

*The Smileys are listed in ASCII sort order. The following is a list of the collating sequence which you may wish to consult. A blank space is sorted before any of the following characters.*

```
!  "  #  $  %  &  '  ( )  *  +  ,  -  .    /
0-9  :  ;  <  =  >  ?  @  A-Z  [  \  ]    ^
_    `  a-z  {  |  }  ~
```

| | |
|---|---|
| - ( | should always wear safety glasses, especially in the laser burn-in room |
| ! - ( | black eye |
| ! - \| | "I-am-a-Cylon-Centurian-with-one-red-eye-bouncing-back-and-forth." |
| ! . ' v | (profile) flat top |
| ! \| : - ( ) | being brained by a baseball bat |
| # ( , ' % / ) | slept too long on one side and didn't have time to wash hair |
| # - ) | partied all night |
| # : - ) | "Everything you know is wrong." |
| # : - ) | for people whose hair is in a mess |
| # : - ) | smiley done by someone with matted hair |

| | |
|---|---|
| **#:-o** | "Oh, nooooooo!"<br>(a la Mr. Bill) |
| **#:-o** | shocked smiley done by someone<br>with matted hair |

> Forgive me if I'm a little
> slow this morning.   %*@:-(

| | |
|---|---|
| **#:o+=** | Betty Boop |
| **$$** | for academic jobs |
| **$$$** | for industrial jobs |
| **$$$$** | for people starting up their<br>own company |
| **$-)** | Alex P. Keaton<br>(from "Family Ties") |
| **$-)** | won big at Las Vegas |
| **$-)** | won the lottery |
| **$-)** | yuppie |
| **%** | for bike accidents<br>(a bit far-fetched, I suppose) |
| **%')** | after drinking a fifth for lunch |
| **%*@:-(** | hung over |
| **%*}** | very drunk |
| **%+{** | lost a fight |
| **%-(** | confusion |
| **%-(I)** | laughing out loud |

| | |
|---|---|
| %-) | Elephant man |
| %-) | after staring at the terminal for 36 hours |
| %-) | broken glasses |
| %-) | cross-eyed |
| %-) | drunk with laughter |
| %-) | long bangs |
| %-6 | braindead |
| %-<I> | drunk with laughter |
| %-\ | hungover |
| %-^ | Picasso |
| %-{ | sad variation |
| %-\| | been working all night |
| %-} | humor variation |
| %-~ | Picasso |
| %\v | Picasso man |
| &-\| | tearful |
| &.(.. | crying |
| &:-) | curly hair |
| '-) | one eyed man |
| '-) | only has a left eye, which is closed |
| '-) | wink |
| ':-) | accidentally shaved off one of his eyebrows this morning |

| | |
|---|---|
| `':-)` | one eyebrow |
| `'~;E` | unspecified 4-legged critter |
| `(` | unhappy Cheshire cat |
| `(!)` | reference to non-Vanderbilt SEC football |
| `($)` | speculation on why Vanderbilt is in the SEC |
| `()` | reference to football |
| `(,'%/)` | slept too long on one side |
| `(-)` | needs a haircut |
| `(-.-)Zzz...` | sleeping |
| `(-:` | Australian |
| `(-:` | left-handed |
| `(-::-)` | Siamese twins |
| `(-:|:-)` | Siamese twins |
| `(-E:` | wearing bifocals |
| `(-_-)` | secret smile |
| `(-o-)` | Imperial Tie Fighter ("Star Wars") |
| `(00)` | mooning you |
| `(8-)` | wears glasses |
| `(8-o` | Mr. Bill |
| `(8-{)}` | glasses, moustache, and a beard |
| `(:    (=\|` | wearing a ghost costume |
| `(:)-)` | likes to scuba dive |

| | |
|---|---|
| **( : +)** | big nose |
| **( : -** | unsmiley frowning |
| **( : - #** | I am smiling and I have braces (watch out for the glare!) |
| **( : - #** | said something he shouldn't have |
| **( : - $** | ill |
| **( : - $** | ill-informed about the Renaissance |
| **( : - &** | Rosicrucian |
| **( : - &** | angry |
| **( : - (** | Sting |
| **( : - (** | frowning |
| **( : - (** | unsmiley |
| **( : - )** | "I never sang for my grandfather." |
| **( : - )** | smiley big face |
| **( : - )** | no hair |
| **( : - )** | surprised |
| **( : - )** | wearing bicycle helmet |

```
Just between you and me,
I hear their stock will
split next month. (:-#
```

| | |
|---|---|
| **( : - \*** | kissing |
| **( : - . . .** | heart-broken |

| | |
|---|---|
| **( : -D** | blabber mouth |
| **( : -I** | egghead |
| **( : -\** | VERY sad |
| **( : -{~** | bald & bearded |
| **( : - \| K-** | formally attired |
| **( : <)** | Rastafari |
| **( : <)** | blabber mouth |
| **( : =)** | TWO noses (?) |

## Star Trek was pre-empted this week.  ( : -\

| | |
|---|---|
| **( : >-<** | thief: hands up! |
| **( : I** | egghead without nose |
| **( : ^ (** | Jack Nicholson in Chinatown |
| **( : ^ (** | broken nose |
| **(@ @)** | You're kidding! |
| **(H f** | Robocop in a hydraulic press |
| **(O—<** | fishy |
| **(V) = \|** | pacman champion |
| **(X0 \| \|)** | double hamburger with lettuce and tomato |
| **( [ (** | Robocop |
| **(^^) y-~~~** | smoking |
| **(x)** | reference to Vanderbilt football |

| | |
|---|---|
| ( \| - \|  **F** | Robocop |
| ( }-8] | left-handed bearded smiley with glasses and headphones |
| ) | Cheshire cat |
| ) 8-) | scuba smiley big face |
| ) : - ( | unsmiley big face |
| ) : -) | smiley big face |
| *!#*!^*&:-) | a schizophrenic |
| ** | for winter sports generally |
| **-( | too many shocks |
| *-( | Cyclops got poked in the eye |
| *-) | shot dead |
| *8-) | Beaker (the Muppet lab assistant) |
| *:* | fuzzy |
| *:** | fuzzy with a fuzzy mustache |
| *:o) | Bozo the Clown |
| *<.'v | (profile) wearing snow cap |
| *<8-)X | party outfit with hat and bowtie |
| *<:-) | Santa Claus |
| *<\|:-) | Santa Claus (Ho Ho Ho) |
| *<\|:-)) | Santa Claus |
| *L* | blotto |
| *\| | for oh what a beautiful sunset |
| +-(:-) | Religious leader |

| | |
|---|---|
| **+- ( : - )** | the Pope |
| **+- : - )** | priest |
| **+ : - )** | priest |
| **+< . ' v** | (profile) knight |
| **+< : - )** | "Peace be upon you, my children..." |
| **+< : - \|** | monk/nun |
| **+< \| \| - )** | knight |
| **+O : - )** | the Pope |
| **, - )** | one eye ... and winking |
| **, - )** | other eyed man |
| **, - }** | wry and winking |
| **, . ' v** | (profile) has short hair |
| **, : - )** | David Ogden Stiers' toupee |
| **, : - )** | shaved his left eyebrow off this morning |
| **-** | Helen Keller |
| **- @=** | messages about nuclear war |
| **- - : - (** | punk rocker (real punk rockers don't smile) (alternate version) |
| **- - : - )** | punk rocker (alternate version) |
| **- )** | Jose Feliciano |
| **- - - . . .** | SOS (variant) |
| **- - - . . . - - -** | SOS (really OSO, but retained anyway) |

| | |
|---|---|
| **-/-** | stirring up trouble |
| **-:)** | has mohawk, no nose |
| **-:-(** | punk rocker (real punk rockers don't smile) |

## I think I've said enough! -=

| | |
|---|---|
| **-:-)** | has mohawk |
| **-:-)** | punk rocker |
| **-=** | a doused candle (to end a flame) |
| **-=#:-)** | wizard |
| **->-** | for airline tickets going cheap |
| **->=:-)X** | Zippy the Pinhead |
| **.'!** | (profile) grim |
| **.'"** | (profile) pursing lips |
| **.'J** | (profile) smiling |
| **.'P** | (profile) sticking tongue out |
| **.'T** | (profile) keeping a straight face |
| **.'U** | (profile) yawning |
| **.'V** | (profile) shouting |
| **.'Y** | (profile) whistling |
| **.'\** | (profile) frowning |
| **.'r** | (profile) sticking tongue out |

- `.'v` (profile) talking

- `.'w` (profile) speaking with forked tongue

- `.-(` always should wear safety glasses

- `.-)` Sammy Davis, Jr.

- `.-)` one eye

- `.-]` one eye

- `...--...` ABBA fan

- `...--...` SOS

- `.....(` Wile E. Coyote after attempt on Road Runner's life

- `.\/` duck variation

- `.^v` (profile) pointy nose

- `._)` suffering from Lorentz contractions (they're coming every ten minutes now)

- `/8^{~` hair line, glasses, moustache, and goatee

```
I'm sworn to secrecy
(:-) :-) :-) :-) :-)),
so here goes...
```

- `/:-|` Mr. Spock

- `/;-)` has one big thick cockeyed eyebrow

| | |
|---|---|
| /\ | for camping and backpacking |
| 0-( | scuba diver with a broken mask |
| 0-) | Cyclops |
| 0-) | arc-welder |
| 0-) | scuba diver |
| 0:-) | angel |
| 2B\|^2B | "Forty Seconal should suffice." |
| 2B\|^2B | message about Shakespeare |
| 3 :-) | Bart Simpson |
| 3:*> | Rudolph the reindeer |
| 3:-o | cow |
| 3:[ | mean pet smiley |
| 3:] | pet smiley |
| 3:o[ | net.pets |
| 4:-) | George Washington |
| 5:-) | Elvis Presley |
| 6\/) | elephant |
| 7:) | Ronald Reagan |
| 7:-) | Fred Flintstone |
| 7:^] | Ronald Reagan |
| 8 | infinity |
| 8 :-) | wizard |
| 8 :-I | net.unix-wizards |

| | |
|---|---|
| 8 ( : - ) | Mouseketeer |
| 8 ( : - ) | Walt Disney |
| 8 ) | frog |
| 8 * ) | glasses and a moustache |
| 8 - # | death |
| 8 - ) | "I was the second gunman." |
| 8 - ) | excited |
| 8 - ) | glasses |
| 8 - ) | swimmer |
| 8 - ) | wide-eyed look |
| 8 - * | just ate a hot pepper |
| 8 - O | "Omigod!!" (done after "rm -rf *") |
| 8 - O | took too many no-doz to work on thesis |
| 8 - P | reaction to College Cafeteria Coffee |
| 8 - S | sees all evil |
| 8 - ] | "Wow, maaan!" |
| 8 - o | Mr. Bill |
| 8 - \| | eyes wide with surprise |
| 8 - \| | suspense |
| 8 : ) | pig |
| 8 : - ) | glasses on forehead |
| 8 : - ) | little girl |

| 8:] | gorilla |
| 8=:-) | Galloping Gourmet |
| 8=:-) | chef |
| 8P | bullfrog in mating season |
| 8^ | chicken |
| 8_) | don't get your nose out of joint |
| 8b | bullfrog in mating season |
| : ) | leper |

## Should I mention anyone else I'm seeing? 8-)

| :###) | Jimmy Durante |
| :$) | Donald Trump |
| :%) | an accountant |
| :%)% | has acne |
| :'( | crying |
| :'-( | crying |
| :'-) | crying with happiness |
| :'O | Bob Hope |
| :'} | Richard Nixon |
| :( | frowning |
| :( | sad |
| :(=) | Jimmy Carter |
| :) | Cheshire cat smile |

| | |
|---|---|
| :  ) | happy |
| :  ) | midget smiley |
| :  ) | salamander |
| : * | kisses |
| : * ) | Ed McMahon |
| : * ) | drunk |
| : * ) | drunk smiling face, for those of us who like get intoxicated before or while reading netnews |

## Okay. I'm sorry. How immature! :)  That better?

| | |
|---|---|
| : * ) | everyman |
| : * ) | smile with moustache |
| : + ( | punched nose, hurt |
| : + ) | Carl Friedrich Gauss |
| : , ( | crying |
| : - | male |
| : - | prolog programmer |
| : - ! | bland face |
| : - " | heavy smoker |
| : - " | pursing lips |
| : - # | braces |
| : - # | mouth zipped |

| | |
|---|---|
| **: -#** | my lips are sealed |
| **: -#** | punched in the mouth |
| **: -#\|** | bushy mustache |
| **: -\$** | "These braces sure do hurt!" |
| **: -\$** | mouth wired shut |
| **: -\$** | sellout (does NOT rhyme with zealot!) |
| **: -\$** | uncertainty |
| **: -%** | banker |
| **: -%** | bearded |
| **: -%** | talking out of both sides of mouth |
| **: -&** | tongue-tied |
| **: -'** | smoker |
| **: -'\|** | has a cold |
| **: - (** | "I will start with those you love most." |
| **: - (** | Drama |
| **: - (** | boo hoo |
| **: - (** | frowning |
| **: - (** | has read too many "smiley" articles |
| **: - (** | mad |
| **: - (** | sad |
| **: - (** | sad face, "that comment makes me sad (mad)" |

| | |
|---|---|
| : - ( | unsmiley |
| : - ( ) | "You backed your car over my toe!" |
| : - ( ) | "You stepped on my toe!." |

> Your school system seems to be more enlightened than ours. : - (

| | |
|---|---|
| : - ( : - ( : - ( : - ! | Taylor Caldwell |
| : - () | I stubbed my toe |
| : - (*) | sick of netnews articles, about to vomit |
| : - (0) | yelling |
| : - (=) | big teeth |
| : - (>~ | "I just washed my goatee, and I can't do nuthin' with it." |
| : - ) | "We are all, each of us, alone." |
| : - ) | comedy |
| : - ) | your basic smiley |
| : - ) | ha ha |
| : - ) | happy |
| : - ) | humorous |
| : - ) | smiley standard |
| : - ) | smiling |
| : - ) | the normal smiling face |

| | | |
|---|---|---|
| : - ) | , | outie belly button |
| : - ) | . | innie belly button |
| : - ) | 8 | Dolly Parton |
| : - ) | ) - : | masking theatrical comments |
| : - ) | ... : - ( ... : - ) ... : - ( ... | |

manic depressive

| | | |
|---|---|---|
| : - ) | 8 - | female |
| : - ) | : - ( : - \| : - ? | Edgar Cayce |
| : - ) | : - ) : - ) | loud guffaw |
| : - ) | : - ) : - ) : - ) | Shirley MacLaine |
| : - ) ! ! ! | | Sam Kinnison |
| : - ) ' | | drooling |
| : - ) ) | | double chin |
| : - ) ) ) | | William Conrad |
| : - ) ) ) | | very overweight |
| : - ) * | | speaks Esperanto |
| : - ) — | | 98-pound weakling |
| : - ) - 8 | | woman with large breasts |
| : - ) - O | | smiling doctor with stethoscope |
| : - ) 8 | | man with bowtie |
| : - ) 8 | | well dressed |
| : - ) = = | | Arnold Schwarzenegger |
| : - ) X | | wearing a bowtie |
| : - ) } | | has goatee/beard |

| | |
|---|---|
| : - ) ~ | drooling |
| : - * | "Oops!" |
| : - * | Oops! (covering mouth with hand) |
| : - * | after eating something bitter or sour |
| : - , | "Hmmmm." |
| : - , | smirking |
| :-) | Jamie Farr (Klinger from M*A*S*H) |
| : - - - - - - ) | big liar |
| : - . ) | Madonna |
| : - . ) | Marilyn Monroe |
| : - / | lefty undecided smiley |
| : - / | skeptical |
| : - 0 | "No Yelling!" (Quiet Lab) |
| : - 0 | orator |
| : - 0 | user can't find shift key |
| : - 1 | bland face |
| : - 6 | after eating something sour |
| : - 7 | smiley after a wry statement |
| : - 7 | smokes a pipe |
| : - 7 | talking out of side of mouth |
| : - 7 | wry face |
| : - 8 | talking out both sides of your mouth |

| | |
|---|---|
| **: - 8 (** | condescending stare |
| **: - 9** | licking its lips |
| **: - :** | mutant |
| **: - :** | toothless |
| **: - <** | frowning |
| **: - <** | moustache |
| **: - <** | real sad |
| **: - = )** | Adolph Hitler |
| **: - = )** | older smiley with mustache |
| **: - >** | biting sarcastic face |
| **: - >** | deformed lips |
| **: - >** | happy |
| **: - >** | hey hey |
| **: - > X = = \|** | smiley formalware |

## The problems will go away if you reboot. :------)

| | |
|---|---|
| **: - ?** | smiley smoking a pipe |
| **: - ?** | smoking a pipe |
| **: - ?** | tongue in cheek |
| **: - @** | "I swear." |
| **: - @** | beard has permanent wave *or* was drawn by Picasso |
| **: - @** | extremely angry |

| | |
|---|---|
| **:-@** | screaming |
| **:-@** | swearing |
| **:-B** | drooling |
| **:-C** | just totally unbelieving |
| **:-C** | really bummed out |
| **:-D** | "I am wearing garters." |

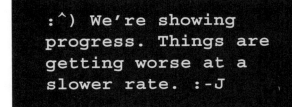

:^) We're showing progress. Things are getting worse at a slower rate. :-J

| | |
|---|---|
| **:-D** | big smile |
| **:-D** | laughing (at you!) |
| **:-D** | said with a smile |
| **:-D** | talking too much |
| **:-D** | wider happy face |
| **:-E** | bucktoothed vampire |
| **:-E** | has major dental problems |
| **:-F** | bucktoothed vampire with one tooth missing |
| **:-G-** | smoking cigarettes |
| **:-I** | "hmm." |
| **:-I** | indifferent |

| | |
|---|---|
| **:-I** | thinking |
| **:-J** | tongue-in-cheek comments |
| **:-M** | speaking no evil |
| **:-O** | Mr. Bill |
| **:-O** | Wow! |
| **:-O** | birth |
| **:-O** | ohh, big mouth, Mick Jagger |
| **:-O** | uh oh |
| **:-O** | yelling |
| **:-O>-o** | American tourist (note big mouth and camera) |
| **:-P** | "I have a longer tongue than Gene Simmons." |
| **:-P** | "Nyahhhh!" |
| **:-P** | has a secret to tell you |
| **:-P** | nyah nyah |
| **:-P** | sticking out tongue |
| **:-P** | telling secrets |
| **:-P** | tongue hanging out in anticipation |
| **:-Q** | smoker |
| **:-Q~** | smoking |
| **:-R** | has the flu |
| **:-S** | just made an incoherent statement |
| **:-T** | keeping a straight face |

| | |
|---|---|
| **:-T** | keeping a straight face (tight-lipped) |
| **:-V** | shouting |
| **:-W** | speak with forked tongue |
| **:-X** | a big wet kiss |
| **:-X** | bowtie |
| **:-X** | my lips are sealed |
| **:-Y** | a quiet aside |
| **:-[** | biting criticism |
| **:-[** | blockhead |
| **:-[** | pouting |
| **:-[** | sarcastic |
| **:-[** | vampire |
| **:-\** | Popeye |
| **:-\** | undecided smiley |
| **:-]** | biting sarcasm |
| **:-]** | blockhead |
| **:-]** | sarcastic |
| **:-`** | spitting out chewing tobacco |
| **:-a** | lefty smiley touching tongue to nose |
| **:-b** | "I have a longer tongue than Gene Simmons, only it is cloven." |
| **:-b** | left-pointing tongue |

| | |
|---|---|
| **:-bill** | Zydeco Bill, with harmonica in mouth and washboard on chest |
| **:-c** | bummed out |
| **:-c** | real unhappy |
| **:-d** | lefty smiley razzing you |
| **:-d~** | smokes heavily |
| **:-e** | disappointed |
| **:-f** | sticking tongue out |
| **:-i** | semi-smiley |
| **:-j** | left-smiling smiley |
| **:-k** | "Beats me, looks like something, though." |
| **:-l** | yet another smiley |
| **:-o** | "Oh, nooooooo!" (a la Mr. Bill) |
| **:-o** | "Oh, the humanity!" |

## Time to take a break. :-O~

| | |
|---|---|
| **:-o** | "Uh oh!" |
| **:-o** | "Wow!" |
| **:-o** | shocked |
| **:-o** | singing national anthem |
| **:-o** | surprise |
| **:-o** | yawn |

| | |
|---|---|
| **:-p** | smiley sticking its tongue out (at you!) |
| **:-p~** | smokes heavily |
| **:-q** | trying to touch tongue to nose |
| **:-r** | sticking tongue out |
| **:-s** | after a BIZARRE comment |
| **:-t** | cross smiley |
| **:-v** | speaking |
| **:-V** | talking head smiley |
| **:-w** | speak with forked tongue |
| **:-x** | "My lips are sealed." |
| **:-x** | kiss kiss |
| **:-x** | not telling any secrets |
| **:-y** | said with a smile |
| **:-z** | yet another cross smiley |
| **:-{** | mustache |
| **:-{** | variation on a theme |
| **:-{#}** | messages teasing people about their braces |
| **:-{)** | moustache |
| **:-{)** | normal smiling face with a moustache |
| **:-{}** | heavy lipstick |
| **:-{~** | has read too many of the toilet paper articles previous to lunch |

| | |
|---|---|
| **: - \|** | "Have an ordinary day." |
| **: - \|** | grim |
| **: - \|** | no expression |
| **: - \| 8 ( ) -** | pregnant |

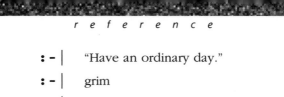

I've been trying to reach you all day. :-|

| | |
|---|---|
| **: - \| : - \|** | dejá vu |
| **: - \| \|** | angry |
| **: - }** | "Thish wine tashted pretty good." |
| **: - }** | beard |
| **: - }** | fiendish grin |
| **: - }** | lipstick |
| **: - }** | pretty lips |
| **: - }** | wears lipstick or some other lip appearance improving device |
| **: - ~ )** | has a cold |
| **: / )** | not funny |
| **: / 7 )** | Cyrano de Bergerac |
| **: / i** | no smoking |
| **: 3 - <** | dog |
| **: 8 )** | pig |
| **: : - )** | wears glasses |

| | |
|---|---|
| `::=))` | double vision or needs new shocks |
| `:<` | midget unsmiley |
| `:<` | "What pretences!" |
| `:<)` | from an Ivy League School |
| `:<)=` | for those with beards too |
| `:<=` | walrus |
| `:<\|` | attends an Ivy League school |
| `:=\|` | baboon |
| `:=)` | has two noses |
| `:=8)` | baboon |
| `:>` | "Hmm, let me think..." |
| `:>` | midget smiley |
| `:>)` | big nose |
| `:?)` | philosopher |
| `:@` | "What?" |

```
/* this code works now
... really :-) */
```

| | |
|---|---|
| `:@)` | pig |
| `:C` | "What?" |
| `:D` | laughter |
| `:I` | "Hmmm, not funny!" |
| `:O` | yelling |

| | |
|---|---|
| **: P** | sticking out tongue |
| **: Q** | smoking |
| **: Q** | "What?" |
| **: Q)** | John Q. Public |
| **: Ui** | smoking |
| **: Uj** | smoking (and smiling) |
| **: V** | woodpecker |
| **: V)** | woodpecker |
| **: X** | lips are sealed |
| **: X)** | hearing no evil |
| **: [** | real downer |
| **: ]** | Gleep...a friendly midget smiley who will gladly be your friend |
| **: ^ (** | has had his nose put out of joint; useful for replying to flames |
| **: ^)** | 3/4 view of person with elf-type sharp nose |
| **: ^)** | broken nose |
| **: ^)** | smiley with pointy nose (righty) |
| **: ^D** | "Great! I like it!" |
| **: ^{** | for those with moustaches |
| **: ^{ ) >** | moustache and beard |
| **: _)** | after a fight where his nose was smashed in |
| **: _)** | nose sliding off face |

| | |
|---|---|
| **:b** | sticking out tongue |
| **:c)** | big nose variant |
| **:c<** | big nose variant |
| **:d** | stick out your tongue |
| **:n)** | funny-looking right nose |
| **:o)** | Stimpy (of Ren & Stimpy) |
| **\*:q** | vi user saying, "How do I get out of this damn emacs editor?" |
| **:u)** | funny-looking left nose |
| **:v)** | left-pointing nose |
| **:{** | "Oh boy, the headmaster!..." |
| **:}** | "What should we call these?" (what?) |
| **:~(** | nose put out of joint |
| **:~)** | Peter Uebberoth |
| **:~)** | needs a nosejob |
| **:~)** | pointy nose (righty) |
| **:~)** | ugly nose |
| **:~-(** | crying |
| **:~-)** | so happy, s/he is crying |
| **:~/** | really mixed up |
| **;** | Cheshire cat with gingivitis |
| **;(** | crying |
| **;)** | winking |

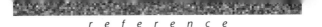

# "Happy Happy, Joy Joy!" :o)

| | |
|---|---|
| **; - (** | "That makes me so mad that if I ever see you I'll punch your lights out" |
| **; - (** | beaten up |
| **; - (** | crying |
| **; - (** | sad face gets his lights punched out |
| **; - (** | sad or mad and got beat up |
| **; - )** | "If you touch my daughter again, they won't be blanks." |
| **; - )** | a practical joker who played one too many and got beat up |
| **; - )** | beaten up |
| **; - )** | pirate smiling face |
| **; - )** | crying with happiness |
| **; - )** | getting fresh |
| **; - )** | sardonic incredulity |
| **; - )** | smiling face gets his lights punched out |
| **; - )** | winking |
| **; - ?** | wry tongue in cheek |
| **; -D** | a friendly, winking, laughing smile |
| **; - \** | Popeye beaten up |

| | |
|---|---|
| **;-\** | Popeye gets his lights punched out |
| **;-\|** | beaten up but silent |
| **;-\|** | no expression face gets his lights punched out |
| **;-\|** | says nothing but still gets beat up |
| **;-}** | leer? (terminal dependent) |
| **;:-)** | really bad toupee |
| **;^?** | punched out |
| **<&&>** | message concerning rubber chickens |
| **<*:oDX** | clown with bowtie and dunce |

**The conference was _last_ week? <:-O**

| | |
|---|---|
| **<:-(** | disappointed |
| **<:-(** | dunce |
| **<:-)** | Vietnamese peasant |
| **<:-)** | dumb questions |
| **<:-)<<\|** | in a space rocket |
| **<:-I** | dunce |
| **<:-O** | "Eeek!" |
| **<:>==** | a turkey |
| **<:I** | dunce without a nose |

| | |
|---|---|
| `<<<<(:-)` | hat salesman |
| `<=` | for messages about housing in the Snow Belt |
| `<@:{(>X` | mustached chinese man with a toupee (also sporting a goatee and a bowtie) |
| `<I==I)` | on four wheels |
| `<{:-)}` | in a bottle |
| `=)` | variation on a theme... |
| `=):-)` | Uncle Sam |
| `=*0` | Felix the Cat |
| `=-O` | the Enterprise |
| `=-O  *    *    *` | the Enterprise firing photon torpedoes |
| `=-O~~~` | the Enterprise firing phasers |
| `=.'v` | (profile) has mohawk |
| `=8')` | Buster |
| `=8->` | a nerd smiley that's unbearably pleased with itself |
| `=:-#}` | punk rocker with a mustache (no such thing!) |
| `=:-)` | hosehead |
| `=:-H` | football player |
| `=:o]` | Bill Clinton |
| `==#==` | railroad crossings |

| | |
|---|---|
| ===:[OO']>:=== | has been railroaded |
| =====:} | snake |
| =^) | Dagwood Bumstead |
| =\|:-) | Abe Lincoln |
| =\|:-)= | Abe Lincoln |
| >%) | Wile E. Coyote |
| >- | female |

> I don't really know where this discussion is leading, do you? >:-)>

| | |
|---|---|
| >-< | absolutely livid!! |
| >-^);> | fish |
| >8O!... | Bugs Bunny with carrot |
| >:) | a little devil |
| >:*) | Bozo the Clown |
| >:-( | mad, annoyed |
| >:-( | sick and tired of reading this nonsense |
| >:-) | devil |
| >:-< | mad |
| >:-> | devilish |

| | |
|---|---|
| **>:-I** | net.startrek |
| **>:-b** | left-pointing tongue smiley |
| **>:^(** | headhunter (Amazon style) |
| **>;-)** | devilish wink |
| **>;->** | winky and devil combined. A very lewd remark was just made. |
| **>< ><** | about/to someone wearing argyle socks |
| **>>-O->** | General Custer |
| **>>>>>:============** | an asparagus |
| **>[I** | Television |
| **>w** | nose-thumbing gesture |
| **>\|(** | Robocop: "Thank you for your co-operation." |
| **?-(** | about people with a black eye |
| **?-(** | has black eye |
| **?:)** | single curl of hair |
| **@%&$%&** | N.W.A. fan |
| **@%&$%&** | you know what that means... |
| **@%&$%&$\&*@%$#@** | and you know what *that* means... |
| **@-(** | "Ulysses! Bring me Ulysses!" |
| **@-)** | Cyclops |
| **@-)** | Space... The Final Frontier |

| | |
|---|---|
| **@-)** | seeing stars |
| **@.'v** | (profile) has curly hair |
| **@:-)** | wavy hair |
| **@:-)** | wearing a turban |
| **@:I** | turban |
| **@=** | "Kafka was a momma's boy." |
| **@=** | flame about nuclear war, power or weapons follows (mushroom cloud) |
| **@=** | pro-nuclear war |
| **@>--->--** | a rose |
| **@O=E<=** | woman in skirt wearing turtleneck sweater |
| **@1@** | too many hours at terminal |
| **B)** | frog wearing sunglasses |

I'll be out of touch for two weeks. See ya! B-)-[<

| | |
|---|---|
| **B-(8** | Sir Robin Day (a British BBC TV presenter, famed for his grumpy countenance, and who wears glasses and a bowtie) |
| **B-)** | "Holy trichinosis!" |
| **B-)** | "I pray daily for death." |
| **B-)** | "Let's do the beach, man!" |
| **B-)** | Batman |

| | |
|---|---|
| **B-)** | glasses |
| **B-)** | horn-rimmed glasses |
| **B-)** | sunglasses |
| **B-)-[<** | sunglasses and swimming trunk |
| **B-D** | "Serves you right, dummy!!" |
| **B-\|** | cheap sunglasses |
| **B:-)** | sunglasses on head |
| **B^)** | hornrimmed glasses |
| **C:#** | football player |
| **C:-)** | large brain capacity |
| **C=:-)** | chef |
| **C=>8*)** | devilish chef with glasses and a moustache |
| **C=}>;*{))** | mega-smiley...a drunk, devilish chef with a toupee in an updraft, a mustache, and a double chin |
| **C=}>;*{O)** | shocked mega-smiley...a drunk, devilish chef with a toupee in an updraft, a mustache, and a double chin |
| **C\|:-=** | Charlie Chaplin |
| **E-:-)** | ham radio operator |
| **E-:-I** | net.ham-radio |
| **EK(** | Frankenstein |
| **Honk!  oo—-oo-Bo** | semi-truck moving right |

| | |
|---|---|
| **Ic:()** | pygmy with bone in hair |
| **K:P** | a little kid with a propeller beanie |
| **K;)B** | seductive woman with bow in her hair |
| **L:-)** | just graduated |
| **M-)** | sees no evil |

## Don't blame _me_ ! O:-)

| | |
|---|---|
| **M-),:X),:-M** | sees no evil, hears no evil, speaks no evil |
| **M.^.M** | nirvana or the failure of a chiropracter |
| **M:-)** | saluting |
| **O 8-)** | the angelic halo look |
| **O :-)** | an angel (at heart, at least) |
| **O \|-)** | net.religion |
| **O+** | appropriate for women's messages, surely |
| **O-&-<** | doing nothing |
| **O-(==<** | chastised and/or chagrined, or is merely asleep |
| **O-)** | Megaton Man, on patrol! |
| **O-)** | cyclops |
| **O-)** | scuba diver |
| **O-G-<** | pointing to self |

| | |
|---|---|
| O-S-< | in a hurry |
| O-Z-< | in a big hurry |
| O:-) | acting very innocent (halo) |
| O>-<\|= | of interest to women |
| OO | headlights on msg |
| P-) | Colonel Klink (Hogan's Heroes) |
| P-) | getting fresh |
| Q:-) | new graduate |
| R-) | broken glasses |
| X-( | just died |
| X-( | net.suicide |
| [8-{) | bearded smiley with glasses and headphones |
| [:-) | listening to walkman |
| [:-) | wearing a walkman |
| [:-] | square head |
| [:] | robot |
| [:\|] | robot (or other AI project) |
| [= | for messages about housing in Arizona |
| [] | hugs |
| \.^./ | lotus position, seen from above |
| \/\/\/\,8-O | really should fix frayed line cord on terminal |

| | |
|---|---|
| `\:-)` | french hat |
| `\:^)` | gumby smiley |
| `\o/` | PTL (praise the lord, or pass the loot?) |
| `\|=//` | George Bush |
| `]:-)` | the Devil |
| `]:->` | the Devil |
| `^(^` | happy variation |
| `^)^   ^(^` | two people talking |
| `^L^` | happy |
| `^v^v^` | mountains |
| `_\\//` | Vulcan salute |

> And I thought that _I_
> was living in limbo! ;-)

| | |
|---|---|
| `__!` | enough for now |
| `__.` | properly chastised and/or chagrined, or is merely asleep |
| `__/~`-'~\_/` | line of thought isn't quite a line |
| `__Q~`__` | cat |
| `_____` | Wile E. Coyote under rock |
| `_____` | a He-Ne laser line |
| `_____` | student EEG on Saturday night |

| | |
|---|---|
| `` `-_-' `` | "Have you hugged your wolf today?" |
| `` `:-) `` | shaved his right eyebrow off this morning |
| `` `^J `` | tongue in cheek |
| `d :-o` | hats off to your great idea |
| `d.'v` | (profile) wearing hard hat |
| `d8=` | "Your pet beaver is wearing goggles and a hard hat." |
| `d:-)` | baseball player |
| `g-)` | wearing pince-nez glasses |

`i-=<*** __.`
CAUTION: has flame thrower and uses it!

`i-=<****** o-(==<`
CAUTION: has flame thrower and uses it!

`i-=<***i`
CAUTION: has flame thrower

| | |
|---|---|
| `o-)` | Cyclops |
| `o-<:-{{{` | Santa Claus |
| `o/` | raised hand |
| `o=` | a burning candle (for flames) |
| `o>-<\|=` | of interest only to women |
| `oCc:-)` | Carmen Miranda |
| `oF-oo—-oo` | semi-truck moving left |

**oO:-)\*\*\*** Santa Claus

    **oO** "It's cold out."

    **oO** somebody's head-lights are on

    **oO-** puzzled, confused

**ouch... O>—<**
    dead driver/passenger on pavement

## My office _is_ my garage. :-o

    **pp#** cow

    **pq`#'** bull

    **q:-)** wearing baseball cap backwards

    **r:-)** wearing ponytail

    **y:-)** bad toupee

    **{** Alfred Hitchcock

    **{** a psycho

**{    :-)** Marge Simpson (Homer's wife)

    **{(:-)** wearing toupee

    **{0-)** Cyclops

    **{8-}** grinning mischievously (or just charmingly)

    **{:-)** hair parted in the middle

    **{:-)** new hair style

    **{:-)** wearing a toupee

| `{:-{)}` | new hair style, mustache and beard |
| `{:\/` | sounds like a duck |
| `{:^=(` | Adolph Hitler |
| `{=` | for messages about housing |
| `{{-}}}` | refugee from the '60's |
| `{}` | no comment |
| `|` | for bike fleet messages |
| `|)` | salamander |
| `|-(` | asleep with nightmares |
| `|-(` | late at night |
| `|-(` | yawn |
| `|-)` | same as :-) but poster is Asian |
| `|-)` | asleep (boredom) |
| `|-)` | hee hee |
| `|-<>` | kissy face |
| `|-D` | ho ho |
| `|-I` | sleeping |
| `|-O` | birth |
| `|-O` | bored |
| `|-O` | yawning/snoring |
| `|-P` | reaction to unusually ugly C code |
| `|-P` | yuk |
| `|-{` | "Good Grief!" (Charlie Brown?) |

| : - )    heavy eyebrows
| : -O    somebody
| : - |    excessively rigid
| : [ `    Groucho Marx
| I    asleep
| ^o    snoring
| |    for messages about cars or other four-wheeled vehicles
| | * (    handshake offered
| | * )    handshake accepted
| ~ (    "Someone just busted my nose."
} ( : - (    wearing toupee in wind
} - )    a wry grin
} : - (    bull headed
} : - (    toupee in an updraft
} : - )    hair parted in the middle in an updraft
} : - <    cat
} : ^#} )    mega-smiley: updrafted bushy-mustached pointy-nosed smiley with a double-chin
} : ~#} )    mega-smiley: updrafted bushy-mustached runny-nosed smiley with a double-chin

## }}\/=oo--oo   Crash!
semi-truck after collision

~ :-(      particularly angry

~#:-(    "I just washed my hair, and I can't do nuthin' with it."

~'v      (profile) has long bangs

~:-(     net.flame

~=      a candle, to annotate flaming messages

~==     flame follows (picture of a lit match or candle)

~M\`'~    camel

~~:-(     net.flame

### I have to go. I have 2000 envelopes to stuff. |-O

~~\8-O    needs to fix frayed cord on terminal

~~~\8-O    zapped by frayed cord on terminal

~~~c____    beach

~~~~8}    snake

~~~~~8}    snake

~~~~~:>    person in a transporter beam

~~~~~>    photon

# Smiley Contest Winners

*Pete "Ender" Walsh of Falls Church, Virginia, has been named the winner of the $500 prize for the best submission to our "Best New Smiley Contest." The 20 runners-up will each receive a copy of the new edition of Ed Krol's Whole Internet User's Guide & Catalog. The contest was judged by David Sanderson, compiler of SMILEYS, and Lesley Strother, a designer at O'Reilly & Associates, Inc.*

## The Winning Entry

### >[:^)

"Watches too much TV"  **Pete "Ender" Walsh**

## The Runners-Up

| | |
|---|---|
| `::-b\|d-::` | "Person with glasses sticking out tongue at mirror'" **Galen Johnson** |
| `=[8]-o` | "Spaceman Spiff preparing to land" **Greg Boyd** |
| `.!!!,` | "Lion hand" **Laszio Drotos** |
| `]:-{o` | "Barbershop quartet singer" **Neil Sokolowski** |
| `<*(:=?` | "Wizard who doesn't know the answer" **Bruce J. Barton** |
| `,,,^..^,,,` | "Cat peeking over a fence (note claws)" **Ina L. Mehlman** |
| `#:o\:o/:o\:o/:o\|\|` | "Totem pole" **Michael Maier** |
| `(:-O ==>` | "Rush Limbaugh (note loud tie)" **Heather Taylor** |
| `(Z(:^P` | "Napoleon" **Paul Curcio** |
| `*-=\|8-D` | "Clown" **Charles Hannum** |
| `:-8p` | "Dizzy Gillespie" **Michael J. Kahlke** |
| `IIIIII8^)X` | "The Cat in the Hat" **N. Murray** |
| `` `,`,`,`,`:\| `` | "Mrs. Frankenstein" **Matthew Allen Lewis** |
| `` `@_____ `` | "Snail mail" **Robert Mudry** |
| `` `\=o-o=/' `` | "Eye glasses" **Jose Manuel Pereira** |
| `oO:)&` | "A grandmother" **Maureen Zapryluk** |
| `/\/:/\"` | "Mummy" **Barry Ackerman** |
| `())=(` | "Wine glass" **Bonnie Petry** |
| `#!^~/` | "'Kissy' profile: hair (a la Archie Andrews), shades, nose, smooch, chin" **Alan Chamberlain** |
| `<0____/\___/\__` | "Worm" **Martin Frischherz** |

# The Smiley Program

I wrote a computer program to select a smiley at random from the list that I've compiled. It 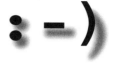 works very simply, as smiley is the name of the program:

```
$ smiley
:->X==|   smiley formalware
```

I use my program to generate a different smiley each day that appear in the prompt on my computer screen. Others use it to add a smiley to the automatic signature line of e-mail messages. The smiley program (with the -l option) also lists all of the smileys that I've compiled. The smiley program is freeware available via

 Internet archives and bulletin boards. The manual page for the smiley program is found on the following page.

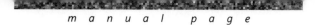

## Name
**smiley** — print or explain smileys

## Synopsis
```
smiley [-V] [-e] [-l] [-f] [smiley...]
```

## Description
*Smiley* is a program for smiley junkies who like to have all the smileys at their fingertips.

The options have the following meaning:

- `-v` Print the version of the program and the number of faces and definitions.
- `-e` Explain the face found in the environment variable SMILEY.
- `-l` Print a listing of all the known smileys, with explanations.
- `-f` Print a random smiley, face only. If given more than once, that many faces are printed, separated by tabs.

`smiley`
   Explain the given smiley.

When invoked with no arguments, *smiley* prints a random smiley with an explanation.

## Example
% smiley -f
:-@    "I swear"
beard has permanent wave *or* was drawn by Picasso.
extremely angry
screaming
swearing